READ TO ME

B287 © 1987 by Jane Dyer

This Book Belongs to

LESLIE CEFALI

A Potter

by Douglas Florian

Greenwillow Books New York

For my
daughters,
Naomi
and Ariel

Black felt pen, crayon,
colored pencils, and
watercolor paints were
used for the full-color art.
The text type is
Bryn Mawr Book.

Greenwillow Books, a
division of William Morrow
& Company, Inc.,
105 Madison Avenue,
New York, NY 10016.
Printed in Hong Kong
by South China Printing
Company (1988) Ltd.

First Edition
10 9 8 7 6 5 4 3 2 1

Library of Congress
Cataloging-in-Publication Data
Florian, Douglas.
A potter / by Douglas Florian.
p.   cm.
Summary: Illustrates what
a potter does with clay.
ISBN 0-688-10100-3.
ISBN 0-688-10101-1 (lib. bdg.)
1. Pottery craft—
Juvenile literature.
2. Potters—Juvenile literature.
[1. Pottery craft.
2. Handicraft.]
I. Title.   TT921.F57 1991
738—dc20
90-33940   CIP   AC

A potter works with clay,

kneading it with her hands,

throwing it on a wheel,

shaping it
with her
fingers,

painting it with glazes,

firing it in a kiln,

making pottery
out of clay and fire.

Jars and jugs.

Cups and mugs.

Bottles and bowls.

Planters with holes.

Plates with spots.

And lots of pots!

Day after day,

by hand or on a wheel,

a potter works
with clay.